THIS BOOK WILL PAY FOR ITSELF

THIS BOOK WILL PAY FOR ITSELF

a non-expert's guide to
managing your money

ANDREW THIES

TATE PUBLISHING
AND ENTERPRISES, LLC

Published by Tate Publishing & Enterprises, LLC
127 E. Trade Center Terrace | Mustang, Oklahoma 73064 USA
1.888.361.9473 | www.tatepublishing.com

Tate Publishing is committed to excellence in the publishing industry. The company reflects the philosophy established by the founders, based on Psalm 68:11,
"The Lord gave the word and great was the company of those who published it."

Book design copyright © 2012 by Tate Publishing, LLC. All rights reserved.
Cover design by Erin DeMoss
Interior design by Lindsay B. Behrens

Published in the United States of America

ISBN: 978-1-61862-843-5
1. Business & Economics / Budgeting
2. Business & Economics / Finance
12.04.24

To my family and friends, who encouraged me to write this book when they said, "Hey, you should write a book about that!" And a special thanks to Roseanne for her extra support and trust in me.

TABLE OF CONTENTS

PART ONE:
Think before You Buy!

Introduction. 11

Food 15

Clothing 29

Electronics. 37

Movies and Music and Books (Oh My!) 43

Vacations. 51

PART TWO:
How to Get the Most Out of the Money You Have

Introduction. 63

Budgeting 65

Other Ways to Save Money 77

Conclusion 93

PART ONE:

Think before You Buy!

INTRODUCTION

Let me start off by saying that this book will not make you rich. I was considering that as a title for this book, but I didn't think it would appeal to people. However, I must say again that this book will not make you rich. It will help you to get more out of the money you have and live better with what you make. And if you learn and practice the things I talk about in this book, it will be all the better for you when you start to make a higher salary some time down the road or your financial situation improves. Then you'll be able to make that extra money go even further. This book will help everybody, whether you're well off or struggling. I've come to the conclusion, however, that most people are not as bad off as they think they are (including myself). It is easy to panic when you start to struggle with or even get behind in your bills. That's when you need to take a moment, breathe, and assess your financial situation. You may realize that you're actually okay and that you just need to start spending your money a little more wisely.

Before I go any further, let me just come clean and tell you that I am not an economics expert. I have no degree in finances or accounting, and I definitely am not independently wealthy by any stretch of the imagination. (In fact, I am actually a poor artist with degrees in commercial and fine art!) I'm just a man who, because he doesn't have a lot, has figured out how to get more out of his money. Everything I'm going to tell you in this book comes from my own experience of living on a very tight budget. What I talk about in this book is not anything brilliant or revolutionary. Most of it is just pointing out the simple things people forget when they're out shopping or trying to budget their money. I'm also simply presenting a different approach to spending and budgeting. It's all common sense. Also, please keep in mind these are methods that I use personally. I will not cover all the possible ways you can save money. But if this book inspires new ideas for you or reminds you of other ways to save money, then it has still done its job!

I can tell you with the utmost confidence that what I've learned and practiced does work. I can even promise that if you apply just one or two of the ideas I present in this book, you will save yourself the cost of the book. You will also notice that throughout the book I try to avoid using any brand names. I didn't write this book to advertise for any particular company. They have plenty of money and highly skilled professionals to market and promote their own brand. They certainly don't need my help! Besides, things change so fast in corporate America that a particular brand or company may no longer exist by the time you read this book. So feel free to insert your own favorite product or service into the strategies I give you.

I have also learned that budgeting is primary and indispensable. You can't keep track of where your money is going and how much you are spending without following a budget. That's what gets most people in trouble. It's very much like dieting. It's not the big meals and general overeating that causes people to gain weight. It's the nibbling here and there that people lose track of that causes the problem. That nibbling can add up fast! It's the same thing with spending. It's not the big purchases that will put you in the proverbial poor house; it's the smaller purchases of three, four, or five dollars that add up to a lot at the end of the month. That's what this book is all about, the little things. Although some things I talk about will save you larger amounts of money, the majority of the book is about saving that little bit here and there that would otherwise add up to a larger sum and bite you in the proverbial butt!

Most of this book is divided into chapters about the different things you spend money on: food, clothes, music, etc. The last part of this book is broader and covers things like budgeting, credit cards, and retirement. The chapters are short and to the point so you can start saving money as soon as possible. None of these chapters are going to tell you how you can get everything you've ever wanted (though it could help you get closer) or how to make more money than you've ever dreamed of. Rather, this book will tell you how to utilize the money you already have more effectively by being smarter about how you spend it. So find a comfortable chair, pour yourself a cup of coffee or a glass of your favorite beverage, and take notes. I sincerely hope you find at least a few things in this book that will help you (if not all of it).

Thanks for buying this book, and I wish you all the best.

FOOD

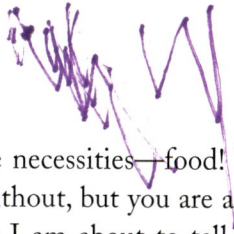

Let's start with one of the necessities—food! There are a lot of things you can go without, but you are always going to have to eat. Now, what I am about to tell you will be repeated over and over throughout this book, but it's a biggie! Always look for sales! Sales! Sales! Sales!

I'm going to begin with your favorite grocery store. At one time or another, almost everything you buy at the grocery store will go on sale. And they go on sale often. Many times grocers stock up on too much of various products and need to move them quickly. The grocer's goof is your gain! You can almost always find something that you regularly buy on sale. When you find such items, buy as much as you need to get you through the next couple of weeks or so. The next time you go shopping you won't need to buy those items. Instead, you can use that money to buy other items you regularly use that might be on sale. Eventually you will get into a rotation where the things you normally buy are either in stock at home, or on sale at the store. It may sound a little complicated at first, but once you get it started, it's very easy to maintain. And it's also fun hunting for the sales! I believe it fulfills that need of the hunter/gatherer in all of us. I usually save 30 to 40 percent on my groceries this way. It may seem like an obvious point to buy things on sale to save money, but you'd be amazed how many people forget to look for sales or even bother with them.

Not all sales are created equal. There are many different types of sales and different ways to use them as well. One of the best sales is the meat sale. Almost weekly, grocery stores will put certain types of meat on sale because they are close to their *sell-by* date. Let me take a moment to explain sell-by dates as opposed to *expiration* dates. Expiration dates are a guide to let you know when a product should probably not be used anymore. I say "probably" because I have consumed food, such as milk, days after the expiration date and had no problems. The food doesn't instantly turn bad on that exact date; it's just a buffer to let you know that the food won't be good for very long after that date. Sell-by dates are set earlier than expiration dates. This serves as an extra buffer to make sure foods like meat are absolutely safe when sold. So you have plenty of time even when a food is close to its sell-by date. The beautiful thing with foods like meat is that you can freeze them. Therefore, class, when they put meat that is close to the sell-by date on sale, you can stock up on that particular meat, provided you have room in your freezer. Now you use the same rotation system as you do with the groceries. Eventually the meat you like will either be in your freezer at home or on sale at the store. And the sales often save you over half of the regular price. Think of it! When you buy something at half off, you're paying the same price people paid twenty years ago. Good deal! Worth the trouble!

Beware of the sales that require you to buy two or three items to get the next one free. In theory you are saving money on all the items if you divide the number of items into what you paid for them. And if it's something you regularly use, those sales are great. But if you don't use that item often or regularly, you can end up wasting money by trying to save a little bit. I have always said that the best way to save money is to not spend it in the first place. (I realized at one point that is a variation of Benjamin Franklin's adage about a penny saved is a penny earned.) Just buy one product and save the money you would've had to spend on the extra two items to get the fourth free. You have to keep your budget in mind for groceries and decide how much you want to spend for that week. If you blow this week's budget on a sale like that, then you have to figure out how to make up for the lost money in the following weeks.

A great way to keep track of sales at your grocery store is online. One of the grocery stores I shop at has a huge program online that works in conjunction with my "savings card." There are several categories that include deals that have automatically been downloaded to my card, deals that I can pick and choose to download to my card, online coupons, and the newest thing they call "hot deals." The hot deals are particularly good buys for that week. I recently bought four pounds of frozen chicken, a gallon of milk, and a half gallon of orange juice for eight bucks! That came to 50 percent off the regular price. The best thing is, I had just downloaded the deals to my card on my smart phone in the frozen section of the store. Ain't technology wonderful! Some of the deals, like the hot deals, are only good for the week, but others can be good for over a month. All you have to do is make your grocery list and then go online and see what items on your list match any of the deals, coupons, or hot deals on the site and download them to your card. The site will then put all those deals on a list for you to print and take with you to the store. You're free of any coupons or sale ads in your hands, with no muss and no fuss! The store will also send you emails when new deals have been added to the site, and there are apps for your smart phone to notify you about upcoming deals as well. You can go to your store's website to sign up or ask at the customer service desk at the store. There are also many sites, not affiliated with any one store, that offer coupons for all kinds of products and services. All you have to do is find the products you want, click on the coupon, and print them out. You can do it through Facebook and Twitter as well, and you can have these sites notify you of new products and deals by email or Facebook and Twitter. At coupons. com, for example, you can hit "local coupons" and it will list deals and coupons for restaurants, products, and services specifically in your area. Other types of sites that offer special deals are sites such as Groupon.com. Here, the deals are only valid if enough people sign up for that particular deal. For example, a car wash place is offering 50 percent off their car washes if at least twenty-five people sign on for the deal. If that happens, the deal is on, and then the car wash place will offer a limited amount of washes for that price for a limited time. You get a good deal, and the retailer increases their volume of sales. As always, be sure to read all the fine print for each deal since each one will have different restrictions. Between online and the weekly flyers sent to you every week from all the grocery stores, you can find plenty of deals, sales, and coupons to save a lot of money.

Think, too, about how you can save money by what type of product you buy. For example, when you buy paper towels, your first thought should be to find the least expensive one. That would be right, but also look at the product to see if it's the same amount of paper towels. Sometimes the cheaper ones have fewer sheets on them. Quality is something to consider with something like this too (especially toilet paper!), because if you have to use more sheets of a thinner or less-absorbent towel, then you have to use more. There goes the savings. Also, now they make paper towels with smaller sheets to use for smaller clean ups. They usually cost a little more, but you use less paper towels, which will save you money. You can apply this logic to a lot of different products. So it's not just always looking for the best price but what is the most economical product.

Rebates on food products are, more often than not, a waste of time. They're usually for a dollar or two, and just the cost of the stamp will take a chunk out of that rebate, not to mention the time it takes to fill it out, send it, and then cash a dollar check. I personally do not bother with rebates except on electronics where you can save a few hundred dollars. Even then, it still doesn't always seem worth the hassle! Coupons can save you a chunk of change too, especially when you use them in conjunction with sales. I'm sure you've seen those people on TV and the Internet who talk about combining coupons with sales on particular items and practically have the grocery store paying them to buy the product. That's practically true if you do it right. Just be careful again of the multiple sales angle or other restrictions on the coupons. Some coupons make you buy a certain variety on a certain day when the moon is at its fullest after the spring equinox! (Okay, I made up the part of the spring equinox.) The best coupons are the ones that just offer a flat money amount or percentage off the product, so stick with those!

Just as important as it is to shop around for the best deals, it's also important to shop for the best stores. Just like sales, not all stores are created (or priced) equally, and there can be vast differences in the prices. The difference can be as much as 60 percent on some items. Compare prices as much as you can and see how different stores vary. You'll probably be surprised that a store you thought was high-end has lower prices than the larger chain stores. If you do shop in those chain stores, don't overlook the store brands. A lot of the time the stores put their name on popular brands to sell them at a lower price. Even generic versions of name brands often come from that very same company. Reading the ingredients will tell you if they're the same or not. This is especially true for over-the-counter medication. Many remedies for allergies, colds, and sinus congestion are way overpriced, namely due to the brand name and promotional costs.

Let me illustrate how you can save money by reading labels. There is a medication in pill form to help you break up mucus in your lungs. I apologize for using mucus as an example, but you'll sure as heck remember the story! The product is a name brand, and at the time of the writing of this book, it cost about thirteen bucks for twenty-four pills. I decided to look at a cough medicine with an expectorant, which cost only seven dollars. I found the exact same active ingredient in the cough syrup as was in the name-brand pill, and it had the same amount of that ingredient in each dose. Now I know what you're thinking: why not buy the cough syrup and save six bucks? Yes, that would be a good savings, but we can do even better, grasshopper! So then I looked at the store brand of the name-brand cough syrup. It had the same ingredient, the same amount of said ingredient, and it was two dollars cheaper than the brand name. Sold! Now I saved eight dollars from the cost of the original name-brand pill form. And the best part is the stuff did the job very well!

Be careful of warehouse stores and shopping clubs. On the upside, these places can save you a lot of money in the long run if you consistently use the products you purchase there. There lies the rub. As you know, you have to buy everything in bulk from these places. You don't buy one cup of yogurt at a time you buy twelve. Again, that's not a problem if you're going to use it up before it expires or not grow tired of it. Dry goods are not a problem, but it's hard to use up large amounts of perishable items unless you have a good-size family or a good-size freezer. And don't forget the annual fee you have to pay to shop at these places. Again, let me stress that I am not knocking the warehouse stores. You can save a lot on your food bill if you utilize these places the right way. I have seen people, however, constantly buy one thing after another from a shopping club and just watch it pile up in their homes. Then they call me and want to know if I'd like to take some of that stuff off their hands. Of course I am happy to help them out whenever they need me. So there's another way you can benefit from warehouse stores. Butter up your single friends who buy their stuff from shopping clubs. They'll eventually be giving you a call!

Restaurants are a hard place to save money, and usually the best way to save money with a restaurant is not to go to one at all. But we all like to dine out, especially me, and I would never tell you to cut out restaurants completely. In fact, one of my favorite things to do is go out to dinner with friends. But you have to show restraint when it comes to going out. Some people eat almost all of their meals out, whether it's fine dining or fast food. That can add up very quickly. Remember, it's not the major purchases that put people into financial difficulties; it's the little things that add up! There are things, however, that you can do to save money when you do go out.

The first thing is go easy on the booze! Alcoholic drinks have one of the highest mark-up percentages. The price you pay for one glass of wine could buy you a whole bottle at your grocery store. You're looking at a 300 to 400 percent mark up. Again, I'm not saying not to drink when you go out to dinner, but if you can limit it to one drink with dinner, not only is it healthier for you, but you can easily save yourself ten or twenty bucks, depending on what you drink. If you want to drink more, you can do that at home for a lot less, and it will be a lot safer for you too!

Order food according to how hungry you are, not what you think you should get because the restaurant has specials or all-you-can-eat deals. The specials, in most cases, are not any cheaper than their other meals they're just dishes that are made for that evening only. Be skeptical when your server suggests something for dinner. They may have a hidden agenda, like a quota to meet with that day's specials. And the all-you-can-eat deals are almost ridiculous. Unless you're a four-hundred-pound lineman on a professional football team, you can't eat your money's worth on those deals, nor should you even try. Even regular meals are more than most people should eat. A lot of times I can only get through half of a regular meal, and because of that, I have a couple more opportunities to save some money. I can either split a meal with a friend who would like the same thing and cut my cost in half, or I can take the rest home and have it for lunch the next day and save myself the cost of that lunch. I know it can seem cheap splitting a meal, but it's just being practical and smart. It's usually too much food for one person, so there's no reason to pay for food you're not going to eat, and it's a healthier decision, because you're eating the amount of food that's right for you. (Not only can I save you money, but I may help you lose a few pounds too!) If you can eat the whole meal or you can use the leftovers for lunch the next day, then that's great. You're not wasting your money. But if not, then it's smarter and less expensive to share. Many restaurants have now gotten smart and are offering smaller portions for a lower price. Look for these restaurants and take advantage of them.

Speaking of lunch, this is an area where you can really save some money. This is a very good example of how the little things can add up. If you buy lunch every day for, on average, five to ten bucks a day, you will spend one hundred to two hundred dollars a month for lunch. How many bills can you pay with that money each month? That would cover my electric, cell phone, and regular phone at least. In a year, that would add up to twelve hundred to twenty-four hundred dollars. You could take that money and put it into savings or invest it in a mutual fund and watch it grow (I'll talk about investing later on.) You could also go on a pretty nice vacation!

You can save a lot of money just by taking your lunch to work whenever possible. Buy some deli meat, bread, and the trimmings for around ten dollars, and you can get three or four lunches from that. Bring leftovers from home or when you go out, and that's a free lunch right there. Sometimes I'll make a full dinner, like spaghetti, and divide it up into several tubs and freeze it. That way I can have those for lunch whenever I want to, and I can get a lot of lunches out of spaghetti. Here's the math: a box of spaghetti can run you eighty-nine cents and a jar of sauce for two bucks. Then divide that into three or four lunches and you have lunch for less than a dollar. Another very inexpensive yet satisfying lunch is soup. If you find it on sale, a can of soup could cost you no more than a dollar or two, and they're like a complete meal. Other than having someone buy you lunch, you can't do better than that. Again, I'm not saying you have to cut out going out for lunch completely, but if you can just cut it in half, you could save yourself quite a bit of money per month.

SUMMARY

- Sales! Sales! Sales! Look for sales and stock up on those items until the next sale.

- Use coupons and rebates only when they are worth it!

- Only buy what you need and avoid the buy-three-to-get-one-free thing if you don't need it. The best way to save money is not spend it, so if you don't need it, don't buy it.

- Shop around for grocery stores that have the lowest prices. You may be surprised.

- Cut back on eating out. When you do eat out, watch the booze and desserts, and try to share a meal when they serve more food than one person can (or should) eat.

- Bring your lunch to work. Leftovers, sandwiches, and home-cooked meals or soup can save you quite a bit of money!

CLOTHING

Again, I start out this chapter with these now familiar words: sales, sales, sales! Whenever you go clothes shopping, the first place you should head to in any store is the clearance rack. The word itself gives me a tingle: *clearance!* Oooo! You can easily find clothes up to 80 percent off on these racks. I can't tell you how many times I have found a forty-dollar shirt for five bucks. Now, granted, they are not always the best-looking items on these clearance racks, which is why most of them are on clearance, but I can usually find something stylish and in my taste on these racks. You have to be patient and look. If there isn't something on there you like, wait until the next time you go shopping. Every store, even the high-end stores, has clearance racks, and if you're willing to wait, you can get name-brand clothing for next to nothing. I always go into a store and find something I like among the new lines, and then I wait. Wait for it to go on sale! I can honestly say that for the last fifteen years I have not bought one item of clothing at retail price. The secret with clothes shopping is waiting. Wait for the clothes to go on sale, wait for them to get to the clearance rack, and even after they're on the clearance rack, if you wait a little longer, they get marked down even further. One time I found an overcoat that I liked on a clearance rack that was over half off. I decided to wait just another week and got it for an additional 20 percent off. You don't always have to wait if you really like the item. If it's on sale and you like the price, go ahead and buy it. But if you can wait a little bit, then you can save some pretty good money.

Something that can help you with your sales timing is shopping online. Just about every store from Target and Sears to Eddie Bauer and the Gap have a website where you can shop, find out what's on sale, or take advantage of special deals. Some of these deals are only online and not at the brick and mortar stores, so you'd have to order online and have the items shipped to you. Look for sites that offer free shipping for any order or for orders over a certain amount. If you have to pay for shipping and that cost takes a huge bite out of the money you saved shopping online, then it's obviously not worth it. The other problem with shopping online for clothes is that it's really hard to tell what the clothes will look like on you compared to the beautiful model that's wearing it on the site. Believe me, I've purchased many an item that looked great on the hunk wearing it online or in the weekly ad, and it ended up looking like a pillowcase on me! Some things, like dress shirts, shoes, and underwear, are pretty safe to buy online, but with other items, you just might want to make that trip out to the store and try it on just to make sure! With that in mind, also know that these sites offer you special coupons that aren't in their weekly ads that you can print out and bring to the store to use. As with the grocery stores, they will also email you or notify you through texts about upcoming sales and special deals. As always, be careful of sites that offer saving programs that you have to pay a monthly fee for or that have a lot of restrictions. Most sites will just send offers and coupons without any obligations on your part.

Another thing to wait for is the seasons—the end of the seasons, I should say. Clothing for a particular season comes out months before that season starts. You can buy swim shorts in March and a fall jacket in the middle of August. The clothing season is different than the meteorological seasons. This is a good thing, because clothes go on sale at the end of their retail season, which is just in time for the real season! Confused? It's simple. By the time the end of the retail winter season comes, it's just in time for the actual winter. Only now the clothes are reduced, so the stores can clear them out for the next season. It's a timing thing. The longer you wait, the more they reduce the prices. Now, if you wait too long the clothing could be gone and the next season's clothing is in place. There is still a black velvet jacket I lament over because I waited just a few days too long to buy it. But you have to be willing to take the chance of losing out on some things to get the best deals. Being a firm believer in divine intervention, I figure if I missed out on something, I wasn't meant to have it anyway. There is always another item that's just as good or even better following right behind. Something else people don't realize is that if you buy something that's not on sale and it does go on sale after you purchase it, you can take it back and ask for the difference. Most stores will honor this, especially if it's within a reasonable amount of time, like a week or so.

Another way to save on clothing is to put your snobbery aside. I know that many people will only buy top designer clothing, and they feel that anything else is a dish rag. That is not necessarily true. They also say that the outrageous price they spent on that clothing is worth it and almost necessary. That's really not true! It is true that a lot of the designer clothing with the higher price tags is higher-quality product, but the prices can still be greatly inflated. And other brands that are not as well known can be of very good quality themselves. I have purchased a lot of these lesser-known brands, and they have lasted me for years.

This saves me money in two ways. I save from the lower price, and I save from the fact that I didn't have to buy new clothes for a longer period of time. Some department stores and the so-called "big box" stores can carry good-quality clothing for far less than the exclusive clothing stores and boutiques. Look for the inexpensive stores whose parent company is a higher-end department store. They carry virtually the same product but under a different name to sell it for less. And even if it's slightly lower quality than the designer name, you have to look at what you need the clothes for to decide what you should spend. Shirts and blouses are the perfect example of this. You don't want to spend a couple of hundred dollars on a shirt that you plan on wearing to a picnic or the ball game. I've seen people do that, and I almost laugh when they spill something on them and get all upset that they ruined an expensive shirt. Now if you want a nicer shirt for a house party or for going out for casual dining, go to a well-known department store. Before you start shopping, however, go straight to the clearance rack, find a nice shirt for more than 50 percent off, and voila you will look great and not have to worry about spilling something on your shirt.

You should also buy less expensive shirts to wear with suits. Only the collar and a little of the front shows, so why spend all that money when people are only going to see 5 percent of your shirt? Now, if you really want to get that designer shirt, shop around for a store that offers the best price. Just like with grocery stores, high-end clothing stores are not priced equally. Each store has his or her own overhead and promotional costs, and you as the consumer always pay for that. There can be quite a disparity in prices among peer clothing stores, so compare several stores before buying. You can also wait for the sales at these stores too! Even the high-end stores have clearance racks! If, however, you walk into one of those stores where you see only five items on display, no prices, and someone in the corner making cappuccinos for you, you know you're in an overpriced store! At that point turn around and run like hell! Well, at least grab a cappuccino before you run!

Here's a broader view of buying clothes that can save you quite a bit of money over time: don't ever buy clothes based only on the fact that they're the latest fad. Not only will this be a money-saving tip but also a fashion tip. Look in anyone's closet (including mine!) and you will find several articles of clothing that will make you say, "What was I thinking!" These are usually items you have worn once or you haven't worn at all, and they still have the tags on them. What you're looking at is not only fashion deficit disorder but also a waste of money! You need to buy clothes that fit you well and look good on your body type. You want to find clothes that have style but are not tied down to a particular period in pop culture. If you follow these rules and don't buy clothes that are trendy, then you will start to have a wardrobe that you can wear for a longer period of time and not have to update every six weeks!

Also, take your time building your new wardrobe. I think the last wardrobe overhaul I did for myself took me almost two years. Why so long? You have to wait for those sales and end-of-season bargains! Plus, you need clothes for the different seasons, especially if you live in the Midwest, as I do. We can have twenty below temperatures in the winter and one hundred plus days in the summer, so I need to find different clothes for each extreme and everything in the middle. So it takes time! Patience, grasshopper, patience! And here's a little organizing tip for you. As you buy new clothing, take the old stuff out of the closet and donate it. At least someone else can benefit from you're fashion faux pas. Just make sure they're in good shape. If not, throw them out! Now don't be concerned that it will take you longer to build your wardrobe, because you're buying clothes that look good on you and will be in style for years to come. They won't be hot right now and then go out of style in a matter of months. At this point in time, I haven't bought myself any clothes for almost a year, with the exception of a small shopping spree in Italy—Oh yeah, I was able to afford a trip to Italy. I'll tell you about that in a later chapter.

SUMMARY

- Sales! Sales! Sales! Be patient and wait for that awesome shirt or pair of pants to go on sale!

- Shop by the seasons. Wait until the end of a particular clothing season to buy those season's clothes.

- Be willing to bypass the designer clothes and the exclusive shops and shop at a discount department store once in a while.

- Think about what you need the clothes for before you buy them. If you're looking for a shirt for the weekend barbeque, don't buy the two hundred dollar designer shirt to wear!

- Wear what looks good on you, not what's trendy. Don't throw your money away because of a fashion brain fart!

- Unless you're 100 percent sure that size-two, sequined, pink tank top looks absolutely brilliant on you, don't buy it unless you can try it on and be sure.

ELECTRONICS

Now I'm going to talk about the more expensive world of electronics. Here is where certain things like rebates and catalogs, which I said wouldn't work with groceries and clothing, will definitely help you. I'll talk about those things a little later in this chapter. The first thing I would like to talk about, you should already know: sales, sales, sales! This is where patience really comes into play, because with electronics, things are constantly changing, and everyone wants the latest gadget yesterday! Well let me tell you something about getting that newest toy right off the assembly line. That new computer, TV, or music device will never be at a higher price than when it first hits the market. After that, it inevitably comes down in price as time passes. That happens without the sales. When the product becomes more available, easier to produce, or another version comes out, the price comes down. So just waiting a couple of months can make a huge difference in the price. Trust me; you don't need the latest version of whatever device just came out right here and now. It will be waiting for you down the road at a much better price and, more than likely, as an improved model! How many people do you know who bought a new electronic thing-a-ma-bob or new software that didn't have all of the bugs out of them yet? Then they had to buy a new device or upgrade the software and ended up spending even more money. Now if they had waited a little while longer, the price would've come down, and the product would've been better, and they would have saved money on both fronts.

A perfect example of what I've been talking about is the flat-screen televisions. When they first came out, one model of the flat screen TV cost fifteen thousand dollars (yes, that's thousands). I thought to myself, *Why would anyone pay the same amount of money for a television that you would pay a good used car?* The following year, the price came down to ten thousand dollars (still the same price for a decent used car at the time). *Now* that very same TV goes for around one tenth of the original price! I can assure you, I was perfectly happy to watch my tube television for a couple of years until the price came down. It really isn't much of a sacrifice. So all this price dropping has happened without the benefit of a sale. Now throw a good 20 to 50 percent off on top of the lowered price, and you can really get a good deal!

Look, too, for close-out deals and floor models. When new models of a particular product come out, that last model gets drastically reduced as a closeout sale. There really isn't a vast amount of difference between the old and new models, and certainly not enough to pass up on a really good deal. Floor models can also be a great deal. They haven't been used that much while they were on display. Most of the time they still have the warranty, and retailers can give you a really good deal on them. If you don't see any floor models on sale, ask a salesperson if any are available. Several years ago I saved about 75 percent on a video camera that was on display, and it still works today. Most electronics will become obsolete before they wear out, but that doesn't mean that they're unusable or don't fit your needs.

Well, I know I talked about rebates in the first chapter, and I know I didn't talk about them in a very positive way. Now I will. Rebates in electronics can save you a lot of money, and it's worth the hassle. Yes, it is a hassle. You can spend some quality time putting together everything you need to fulfill the requirements demanded of your basic, standard rebate. Keep the receipts! For the love of God, don't lose the receipts, and be sure to make copies of them. Also keep any and all serial numbers off of the box. Usually you need to have photocopies of those numbers as well when you're sending in multiple rebates for the same product. Follow the rebate instructions very carefully. Have all your papers in order, and have all your t's crossed and all your i's dotted. Miss just one step, and civilization as you know it will come to an end! Okay, civilization will still go on, but it will delay your rebate if you miss anything. There is also usually a time limit for the rebate, so be aware of that too. If you don't process the rebate correctly the first time, you may not have time to fix it. But if you've done everything right, you can save several hundred dollars. I saved three hundred dollars in rebates the last time I bought a computer. I think it was maybe an hour or two of work to get everything together for the rebate. That works out to at least one hundred and fifty dollars per hour for my time! Everyone reading this book right now that makes that kind of money, raise your hand. That's what I thought.

Shopping online is great way to find computers and electronics. Unlike clothes, you don't have to try on a laptop to see if it's right for you. Of course, all the electronics places have websites to shop online and offer deals. Places like Best Buy and hhgregg offer weekly deals, special online deals, and online reward programs. Just read carefully all the details involved with any rewards or savings programs. You'll see a lot of asterisks next to offers, so be sure to read the fine print. These places also offer free shipping and free shipping to a store near you so you can go pick it up yourself. You do, however, need to know what you want and need as far as size, power, capabilities, and all that, which is especially true for computers. You need to know something about computers if you're going to order them online. You're not going to have that slightly arrogant, techno geek there to answer all your questions. So if you know someone who knows anything about computers, start interrogating them for every bit of information. If you do your homework, you can save a good amount of money shopping online and checking through those weekly ads.

At one point in planning this book, I was going to suggest that you look at used and refurbished computers for deals. Maybe find one that's a year or two old. But at the rate that computers become obsolete, it's really not worth it for the most part. The computer will be almost useless as soon as you plug it in. There are exceptions, depending on what you need the computer for. Sometimes people just want to use a computer for the household budget and taxes. Programs for these kinds of functions are upgraded regularly, but the changes aren't as drastic as with other types of programs. You can use the same budgeting program for quite a while on the same computer without needing to upgrade either one. Another case for used computers is small children. I have friends who got a refurbished laptop for their kids when they were around four and six to play games on and to use educational programs. They even got online with it (with all parental controls in place, of course), and it worked great for them. Believe me; a five-year-old does not need umpteen gigabytes of storage and the fastest processor on the planet to make him happy. As long as they can play their favorite games or listen to their favorite tune, they're golden!

SUMMARY

- Sales! Sales! Sales! I can't say it enough!

- Wait for the prices of new electronics to come down on their own.

- Look for close-out deals and floor models. If you don't see them, ask!

- Practice safe rebating! Fill out the rebates carefully, and you can get back a good amount of money.

- Weekly ads and online deals can be your friends. Just be sure you have your facts straight before you hit that send button.

- If you're getting a computer for the kiddies, consider a used or refurbished computer. They can't handle all that power anyway.

MOVIES AND MUSIC AND BOOKS
(OH MY!)

Before getting into this chapter, let me emphasize that I am not trying to discourage you from buying books and music. I love buying these things and have quite a collection, especially books. I just want you to make sure you buy what you really want and get it for a good price. The first thing that applies to all three is yes, say it with me: sales, sales, sales! Sales and also patience, which go hand in hand. You don't have to get the latest movie, CD, or book the day it comes out (with the exception of a certain book about a certain wizard!). Wait! Wait for it to go on sale! The entertainment business makes enough money off of us as it is. We don't need to throw more money than necessary at them! Make them sweat it out a little. They will still make their fortune, so don't worry about them.

With CDs there are two reasons to wait. One is the sale thing: the CD either goes on sale or naturally comes down in price as they always do. The other is to find out if you like the CD or not. So many people will hear the first hit off an album and buy the album based on that one song. The only problem is, what if the rest of the album stinks?

The Internet, once again, is a great way to avoid this terrible fate. Sites like iTunes as well as many others have made it possible to listen to and purchase songs individually from the Internet and download them to your computer, iPod and other devices. This way, you get to listen to the songs first before you buy, and you only have to buy the songs you like from any one album. It's a win/win situation for everyone. The artist and record companies still get their money, and you get exactly what you wanted. You can create a play list for your iPod or mp3 player or burn a CD and create the perfect CD that's actually less than a commercially produced CD. There are also websites like Pandora that are basically radio on the web. The great thing is that you can choose the songs to listen to by title, artist, and even genre. Type in Broadway showstoppers and you start hearing the great Broadway hits! They also list other songs and artists that are similar to the ones you pick. You can use the site to find music you like then go to a site like iTunes and buy the music or, if you prefer, out to the stores and buy the CD. If you don't have Internet access or are still not comfortable with it, you can always head down to your local library. Many libraries have large selections of CDs to lend out. You can check out a CD for a couple of weeks, see if you like it, and then head out to the store and buy it knowing full well what you're buying. You can also use the library's Internet to find the music you want and purchase it. Don't worry; there will be people there to help you! Again, if you're not up for using the web, head out to the big box stores where they still have huge sections of CDs at really good prices. Look for compilation and "best of" albums of your favorite artists or genres of music. They're usually some of the lowest-priced CDs in the store, and they have all the songs you want on one album. You don't have to buy five or six CDs to get all the songs you want. It's easier to determine whether or not movies are worth buying. First of all, you can see them in the theatres when they come out and determine if you like them or not. While we're talking about going to the movies, let me give you a tip on saving a little money here as well. The price of a movie at a first-run theatre is now in double digits. If, however, you wait to see it at the second-run theatres (or the cheapie theatres, as we used to call them), you can still see a movie on the big screen but save over half the ticket price. Now it costs you even less to see it in the theatre, and you can say to yourself, "Yeah, I'll buy that when it comes out on DVD," or "No, once is enough!"

The criterion for me to buy a movie on DVD is whether or not it's the type of movie I want to watch over and over again. Obviously, if it sucks, the decision is made, but sometimes even a good movie is not always the kind of movie you want to watch more than once or twice. Think about things like that before you run right out and buy a DVD. Now let's say you didn't get a chance to see that movie either in the first-run theatre or the cheapie one. What are you going to do? Of course, jump online. There's no shortage of sites like Amazon.com that offer streaming video of DVDs to rent. If you like it, you can then buy it and download it right then or have them ship the copy to you, often with free shipping. If you just want to rent movies or any of the television series on DVD, there are services like Netflix and Blockbuster where you can rent through the mail or download rentals through your computer or TV. You pay a low monthly fee, and you can rent as many DVDs as you can watch each month. This could end up equaling pennies per movie or show. You could replace having cable by using one of these services. Most of the shows on cable are available on DVD, as are the movies. Rent the shows and movies that you actually want to watch for a fraction of the cost of cable or satellite TV. Again, if you don't have Internet access, there is an army of vending machines like Redbox to rent DVDs. They're everywhere. I'm surprised my dentist doesn't have one in his waiting room. The DVDs usually only cost a dollar. You could find that much change in your couch! If you don't even want to dish out a buck for a movie, then head to the library.

More and more libraries have movies to check out, and the larger libraries usually have the latest ones. So now you've seen the movie and you're ready to buy it. Do you run right out and get it? No. Do you wait for it to go on sale? Yes! It's easy for me to wait to buy movies, because I have so many that I haven't even watched yet! Many of them still have the wrapping on them. That's something else to think about before buying a movie. Are you going to watch it in the near future? If not, then wait to buy it. Again, the best way to save money is not spend it in the first place. You may decide you really didn't want the movie, and you will have saved yourself the price of that DVD.

Let's move on to books. What's the best way to save on books? You already know the answer by now, so I'm not even going to tell you. Advancing on, let's talk about bargain books. Many chain booksellers have bargain sections with books covering almost every subject fiction and non-fiction. They are either well-known books that have been reduced because they have been out for a while, or they are books that are published specifically to be inexpensive. You'll notice by now that I try not to use the word "cheap" or "cheaper" as much as possible. Remember, we're not being cheap. We're being frugal! Another thing you'll find on the bargain tables are compilation books. Either they are compilations of famous contemporary authors both fiction and non-fiction or they're classic authors like Dickens and Hemingway. Sometimes they create a series of these books in which each has five or six of the author's best novels. Now if you bought each one those novels separately for thirteen dollars or so, you'd spend about sixty-five to eighty dollars. You can save even more with the contemporary authors. These are not condensed books either. They're the full versions of each book in the compilation. Not only do these books save you money, but they save you space as well. There's another organizing tip for you, free of charge.

Of course, you can't talk about books without talking about websites like Amazon.com and BarnesandNoble. com. Now they have been around for a while, but what they offer and the technology that's available now has skyrocketed in just the last few years. As always with these sites, you can find great prices for just about any book that has been published, especially the latest releases. These prices can be half of the hardcover list price in the store, and you can get deals on books that haven't been released yet. But now with the arrival of electronic readers like Nook and Kindle, these sites also offer downloadable books at even better prices. If you join as a member, Amazon will lend you books to your device from their own library, or you can borrow online books from your local library for free. Some sites will offer books that are in the public domain to download for free. We're talking classics like *Pride and Prejudice* and books written by that Dickens fellow.

A somewhat-famous group from the sixties sang about wanting to be a paperback writer. You may want to consider being a paperback buyer! Paperbacks can be a fourth of the price of a new-release hardcover, and just about every book that comes out ends up being printed in paperback. I realize that there are a lot of people who like to have the hardcover versions of their favorite books or authors. I, too, have my favorite books that I prefer in hardback, like that certain wizard I mentioned earlier and a certain horror writer whose last name rhymes with "ding." But for the books that you don't particularly care either way, definitely wait for the paperback version. They're also more convenient for reading when you're on a train or plane or when you're on vacation. Sand and hardcovers don't mix very well.

I also love going to bargain bookstores. You know the ones that are usually in a strip mall somewhere with the store name on a banner out front in lieu of a real sign? If you don't mind the fluorescent lighting, handwritten signs, and used shopping bags that they put your purchases in, these places are for you! They have new and used books for sale, and the used books can be as low as fifty cents! Of course, with bargain stores as well as the bargain table, you may need to hunt a little bit for a particular book that you want. Again, this is a way to satisfy our hunting instincts that have waned over the millennia!

And finally, if you really don't care about owning the book and just want to read it, where can you possibly go? Oh yeah, the library! They have books, don't they?

SUMMARY

- Sales! Blah! Blah! You know!

- Make sure you like the music or movie you're buying by trying it out first through iTunes or Pandora.com and borrowing from libraries.

- If you want to see a movie in the theater, wait for the second-run theaters. If you want to watch it at home, rent from Netflix for a monthly fee or for a buck from a Redbox.

- Look for compilation CDs and books.

- Shop the bargain tables at chain booksellers and bargain bookstores.

- Don't forget the library!

VACATIONS

Yes, even when money is tight, you can still go on vacation! Besides traveling the country from one end to the other, I've been to Europe several times. Here's how to do it. There are three ways to save money with vacations: stay at home, find a less expensive destination, or find a way to cut the costs of the vacation you're already planning. Let's start with the last one on that list. There are a lot of ways to trim the vacation budget; you just have to be smart about it and be a little tenacious. You really have to hunt for the deals, and there are many ways to do that.

The biggest expense with a vacation, obviously, is the actual traveling expenses, especially airfares. A good place to start finding bargains for those is online. I have used the Internet to find airfares and hotel reservations and was happy with the results. You can do a lot of comparison shopping quickly and easily, giving yourself more options. This is really handy with airfares, because as you know, the fares change every five minutes! Getting the best price takes timing and luck. There are plenty of websites that can help you get the best fares, but be aware of the restrictions. Some sites offer great deals, but you won't know exactly when you're leaving or on what airline until you book the flight. Look for the sites that let you see all the information before you commit to booking the flight.

There are also sites that let you enter a price you're willing to pay. If it's out there, they'll find it or something close to it. Don't book it yet, though. Now you pick up the good ol' telephone and call the airlines and tell them you found this great price online and you're wondering what they can do for you. If they can do better, book it right then and there; if not, go back to the website and book it through them. As I said, it's a timing thing with getting a good deal. You can also find better prices as you get close to your departure date. Airlines will cut prices for a flight close to its departure time to make sure they fill the plane. It's cheaper for them to fly a full plane rather than half full! If you wait too long and get too close to the departure date, you may actually pay a higher fare. That usually happens when you book within ten days of departure. Call the airlines to make sure what the best time is to book and see if they can help out with finding a deal. Like I said, the airlines have the same philosophy as the theater business: get the butts in the seats!

So you have your airline tickets; now you need to get a room (so to speak). Obviously, the best scenario, if you have friends that live where you're vacationing, is to stay with them! It won't cost you anything except a very nice thank you gift or dinner! If you don't have friends living where you're going or they won't let you stay with them because of reasons I'm sure are not your fault, then you can find a hotel the same way you found your airfare. There are plenty of websites to help you find hotels and find reasonable rates, only there aren't the restrictions that you find with airfare websites. Can you imagine if the website wouldn't tell you what hotel you were staying at or when it was available until you booked it? I shouldn't speak so soon; that might still happen.

What I also like about hotel websites is that they can show what the room will look like, tell you what the rates are for weekdays and weekends, and list all the amenities that come with the room. You'll notice I mentioned rates for weekdays and weekends. You may not know that most hotels charge more for Friday and Saturday nights than the other nights of the week. They will, however, give you better deals on packages if you include a weekend night. And, of course, if you go on vacation with someone else, you can save even more by sharing. The more people you have, the more you save. So if you can get a small group together to take a trip, especially to another country, you can cut the hotel cost by 75 percent if you share four to a room. Don't get caught up with all the frills that will cost you extra money. Some hotels have workout facilities, kitchenettes in the rooms, and other things that run up the room rates.

Now, depending on what kind of vacation you're taking, you may want these things. Pools when you're staying in Florida or Arizona are definitely good things to have. But if you're going to New York City I don't know about you, but I'm not exactly going to worry about working out or cooking breakfast in my room. If you're traveling abroad, like to Europe, then heck, all you need is a bed and a pillow. You have a whole world to explore, and you're not going to spend a lot of time in the room. Actually, that's a good thing to remember any place you go. The hotel is the place where you get some sleep; don't make it the focal point of your vacation. Just make sure it's clean, in a good area, and located close to the places you want to visit. You can find all that information out on the websites.

One more tip for you vacationers out there: if you've flown somewhere for your vacation and it's a relatively short trip (one to three hours), plan to return home in the evening rather than in the morning. If you plan to leave for home first thing in the morning on your last day, then you end up paying for that night before just so you can spend the next day traveling. Leave in the afternoon or early evening of your last day, and you save yourself the cost of that night's stay.

So you have the airline tickets and the hotel, and now you need to find things to do while still saving money. There are plenty of ways to do that. Let me give you an example by telling you about my many trips to New York. I always go with my best friend, so we share the cost of the room, which is usually at a good price that she found online. She also always finds really good deals online for airfares. The first thing we do is go to a place that we found on our first trip there that has the cheapest eats in town, and it's good too. They also have giant frozen margaritas! The last time I was there you could get a complete chicken dinner for about eight dollars, which is nearly impossible in New York.

Then we get tickets to a Broadway show. I know you're saying to yourself, "What? Tickets to a Broadway show? Aren't those expensive?" Normally, yes, tickets to a Broadway show are over a hundred dollars, but there is a shining star in the middle of Times Square that can save you lots of money, and it's called TKTS. TKTS is a booth in the middle of Times Square that offers day-of tickets at prices 25 to 50 percent off. All theatres that participate in the program bring tickets for that day to TKTS about four hours before curtain, whether it's a matinee or an evening performance. They discount the tickets anywhere from 25 to 50 percent, depending on the show and the day of the week. I wanted to see *Rent* one year, but it was always just 25 percent off. Then I checked on a Sunday and found it was 50 percent off. If you find an off-Broadway show, you'll save even more, since the ticket prices are a lot less than Broadway shows. On one trip my friend and I got TKTS tickets to an off-Broadway show (which was actually quite close to Broadway) and ate at a nearby pizza parlor. The dinner and show ended up costing a grand total of forty dollars for each of us! In New York, that's practically free!

Do a little research on the place you're going to visit. You can go to the local library and find books on just about any place you're going to or sit in a bookstore/coffee shop and browse through an even wider selection of books on your destination. Look for all the points of interest to visit, but particularly the ones that cost little or no money. Again, I'm not saying you can't spend money on things to do, but there a lot of things to see and do that people don't think about and cost next to nothing. You can visit historic landmarks, museums, and parks just for starters. State and federal governments or non-profit organizations usually fund these places, so the fees are low or non-existent.

You can also visit well-known public places. A good example is New York again. You can go and walk through Times Square, one of the most famous places in the world, for free. Washington Square and SoHo are also great places to go and stroll around and take in the atmosphere. I've done that in Las Vegas as well. We would take a day off from gambling and go see Hoover Dam and Lake Mead, and it cost practically nothing. Sometimes events pop up that you weren't planning on. On my first trip to New York, I was just exploring and enjoying Times Square when I realized they were having a concert smack in the middle of Broadway and 42nd street with all the Broadway performers that were currently in shows. Yea me! Free concert in the middle of Times Square! So keep your eyes open for those unexpected surprises, and do your homework, because a little homework can save you a lot of money.

I have one last money-saving tip for you about vacations: try to be discriminating when buying souvenirs. You really don't need to buy the first thing that has the name of the place you visited slapped on the front of it. Now at this point I should say that I usually buy one of my friends a cheesy souvenir gift each time I go somewhere, but it's definitely for the humor of it. I warn you about these kitschy items, because when you're on vacation and you see these things, they seem fun and look like things you would wear or put on your shelf at home. Then you get them home and you realize how cheap or tacky they are and never look at them again. Then you realize you've wasted your money that you could have spent on something a lot better. I think you get the idea.

When you shop for souvenirs and come across something you think you'd like, take a second to think about whether you really want it, will wear it, or even want to display it! Be honest with yourself, and then decide whether you really want it. (Hmm... this all sounds familiar, doesn't it?) It may very well be that you do want and will wear the oversized t-shirt with the picture of Mt. Rushmore plastered across your chest. That's great, as long as you wear it and you haven't wasted your money! For me, I try to find something that represents what the place is all about. When I was in Assisi, Italy, I bought a cross of St. Francis and a necklace with the cross he designed. I took a pass on the St. Francis potholders and tea cozies! The other thing I bought was a great pair of leather shoes from a little shop in the middle of town. And yes, they were on sale! Sometimes a souvenir can be something that doesn't cost any money, like a program from a Broadway show or a brochure from a historic site. In Ireland, I grabbed coasters from all the pubs I went to (and there were many!). So before you grab that plastic replica of Michelangelo's *David* or a snow globe of Washington DC, take a moment to think about it first and decide if it's going to end up in a shoe box in your closet for the next ten years!

SUMMARY

- Get online to find deals for airfares and hotels.

- Find discounts and less expensive alternatives for things to do on vacation.

- Research your destination to find places and events that are free.

- Make sure the souvenirs you buy are ones you'll actually use, wear, or just enjoy!

PART TWO:

How to Get the Most Out of the Money You Have

INTRODUCTION

Well, if you've made it this far, I thank you very much! If you've tried any of the ideas that I talked about in the first half of this book, then hopefully you have saved some money already. Yea for you! If you've saved the equivalent of the cost of this book, then you've at least broken even. Congratulations! Trust me keep using the ideas in this book, and you'll save a lot more! I talked about how to save money in the first half of this book, and now I want to use the second half to talk about how to handle it and what to do with it. Everything I'm telling you is what I've learned from my own experience, and it has worked well for me. Not everything will work for everyone, but I think there are enough ideas and strategies to help everyone quite a bit.

I'll talk first about the most important thing, which is budgeting! Even if you don't use anything else from this book, if you make and work with a good budget, you will automatically have more money in your pocket than you did before. The secret is sticking to the budget. That is really important, and failing to stick with it is most people's downfall. I cannot stress how important a budget is, but I'll try in this second part!

Next, I'll talk about credit cards and things you can do to not only control them but to save some money with them too. I used the word *control* because it's the most accurate word to use when talking about credit cards. People get themselves into tremendous debt because they lose control over their credit card spending. There are many things you can do to gain control over and manage your credit card debt, and some of those ways involve how you buy and what you buy! You can also save on the interest rates on your cards too!

And then after all of that and you've read through this whole book and you've hopefully saved tons of money we're going to take some of that money and start building a retirement plan. You have to think about the future and decide how you want to live when you retire. And you need to start working on it now!

So bring your tray to the upright position, fasten your seatbelt, and let's continue the ride through the second half of this book!

BUDGETING

Make sure that if you only take one thing away from this book, it's this wise piece of advice: *you cannot manage your money without a budget!* Now close this book for a moment and let that statement sink in a little and then continue reading. Go ahead; I'll wait.

Oh, hi, you're back! Let's continue. You have to learn to make and follow a budget; otherwise, everything I've talked about so far and will talk about in the rest of this book will be for naught! "How does one make a budget?" you ask with dread and hesitation. Fear not, grasshopper, it's simpler than you think. We're going to first create a monthly budget for your bills, and then we'll create a weekly budget for things like food, gas, and entertainment. We'll start with the monthly budget.

The first thing you need to do for a monthly budget is to determine how much you take home per month. I know this sounds obvious, but be sure you calculate the take-home amount of income for the month. I've seen people try to budget with their gross income and then become confused when they're short money at the end of the month. Now take that amount and put it to one side for now.

Next, add up all your fixed expenses for the month. These are the expenses you have to pay a fixed amount on each month. Rent or mortgage, car payments, and insurance premiums are all amounts that don't change from month to month, or at least not until inflation rears its ugly head. After you add those payments up, take a look at your flexible expenses. These are expenses such as gas, electric, and water, which change from month to month depending on usage. Later on we'll talk about how to save money by reducing your usage of things like gas and electricity. (This is where conservation is not only good for the environment but also good for your wallet!)

Credit card payments can be a flexible payment as long as you at least pay the minimum. This payment you have some control over, and you can adjust it to fit your budget each month. Try to pay as much as you can each month, and if you can keep that amount consistent, then that's the amount you can use for your budget. Since other flexible payments change from month to month, like the gas or electric bill, you're going to have to estimate the amount per month when figuring your budget. Try to estimate on the high end to give yourself a little wiggle room. If you overestimate the payments, then you have some extra money, but if you underestimate, then you have to find that extra money! While I'm on the subject of credit cards, here are some ways that I found work best to gain control of your credit card debt. One thing you can do right away is call the credit card companies that you have cards with and ask them to lower your interest rate. You should not be paying higher than 18 percent rates anymore. Ask them to lower it at least five percentage points if you are paying that high of an interest rate. Sometimes they will stonewall you and tell you that there's nothing they can do about the rate, but keep pressing. Tell them that you have offers from other cards at much lower rates. (I'm sure you have received dozens of offers from other cards, so you won't be lying!) More often than not, they acquiesce and offer you a lower percentage rate. The exception to this is if your credit score is too low.

Most of the time your rate is determined by how good your credit score is. If it's high, then your rate is low. If it's low, then your rate is high! It doesn't get any simpler than that! If they don't help you out, then transfer your balance to another card with a lower rate and cancel the higher card. Any amount you can save in interest rates means more money that's applied to the principle balance. Be sure to transfer the balance before you cancel. Many cards have policies that raise your rates as high as 27 percent when you cancel their cards with an existing balance. If you can, transfer any credit card balances you have to one card that has the lowest rate. It's important to then cancel some of the other cards and get rid of them. Consolidation doesn't work if you start running up the balances again on the other cards.

You'll note that I said "some" of you're cards. Sometimes when you cancel cards it can hurt your credit score. If, however, you have too many open accounts, that can hurt your score as well. You have to find the happy medium. Also, call your credit card company when they impose a late fee on you and ask them to remove it. They usually will do this for you if you haven't been late too often with payments in the past. I had two card companies do that to me in one month, and I called both of them to remove the charge, and they did. I saved almost eighty bucks with just two phone calls. Sometimes they will offer to take half of the fee off. You can try to push for the full amount, but that may be all you get!

Another way to keep on top of your credit cards is to always try to make your monthly payments equal to what you charged that month on your card plus the interest. That will, at the very least, keep you from increasing your credit card debt. If you can, make the payment amount you budgeted for plus what you spent that month. That would help you start whittling down your debt. So let's say you've budgeted one hundred and fifty dollars a month for your credit card payment and then you charge another one hundred dollars on your card that month. You should try to make a two hundred and fifty dollar payment on your card to stay on top of your credit debt and continue to chisel away at it. I know this is not always possible, but make every effort to at least pay off what you charged that month plus the interest to keep your debt from getting out of hand.

Of course, if you don't use your card, then most of your payment goes toward reducing the debt, which brings me to my last piece of advice on credit cards: barring any emergency, like medical costs or car repairs, if you can't afford to buy something with cash, then don't buy it! It goes back to my other brilliant saying about the best way to save money—don't spend it in the first place. The same applies to credit cards. The best way not to add to your debt is not to use your card in the first place! Think of your credit card debt as your weight and you're trying to lose some of that weight. You know in weight loss that the basic secret is that more calories need to go out (burning) than come in (eating). It's the same with your debt. More money needs to be coming off your debt (payments) then going in (charges).

Now add the set expenses with the flexible payments, and that's the amount that is going out every month for your bills. Now divide that amount by the number of paychecks you get per month. If you get paid once a week, then that's about four checks per month, and you would divide the expense amount by four. If you get paid every two weeks, then you'll divide by two. If you get paid once a month, well then, have fun trying to budget! Actually, getting paid once a month makes monthly budgeting very easy but weekly budgeting a bit of a challenge! The number you get after working your remedial division problem is the amount you should set aside from each check and put into your checking account.

Again, to some of you reading this right now, this seems like an obvious point, but I know a lot of people who assign each check to a different expense. They apply this check for rent, this check for a car payment, and so on. The problem is that it's very hard to follow the budget this way. If you end up using a whole paycheck to cover some of your bills that week, what are you going to do about food or gas? Maybe from the next paycheck you don't have to save as much, but now you have to use that extra money to make up for the week before. You may have to make that money stretch for a couple of weeks, because you'll be using the next paycheck for another bill. You're either in the hole one week, or you have to try to stretch a check over several weeks. It's best to divide the monthly expenses up over the number of paychecks so there is a consistent amount of money being set aside and a consistent amount of money for weekly expenses. It's just like those charts you see on financial reports on the news. They show you a picture of a dollar, and then they divide the dollar into pieces, showing you what percentage of each dollar goes toward what part of the budget. Now think of your paycheck as that dollar, and each part of that check goes toward the different parts of your budget. Part of it goes for a percentage of your rent or mortgage, and part goes for a percentage of the car payment, and so on and so on.

In terms of actual dollars, it would look like this: if your rent is eight hundred dollars a month and you get paid four times a month, then you would need to take two hundred dollars out of each paycheck that month. Don't devote a whole check and perhaps part of another one to pay the rent when it comes due; otherwise, you have no money for that week and a half. That's when you'll start using the credit card more often, or if you get paid twice a month you'll dip into the second week's budgeted amount, and you get further and further behind. You can end up at a point where you are so far behind you will not be able to get out from under it without some major financial help that could be some generous friends or family, or it could, at the other end of the spectrum, mean filing bankruptcy. Fortunately, I can't tell you much about bankruptcy, because I've never gone through it, and if you pay attention to this book and follow it, you probably will never have to either!

So the budget for all the expenses that you have to pay each month is in place. Now you need to estimate your out-of-pocket expenses. These are things like gas for the car, groceries, entertainment, and anything else that comes up during the week. The best way to calculate this is to keep all the receipts of everything you spend money on during the week or at least write down everything you spend each week. Do that for a month, add up all the weeks, and that will give you a good indication of how much you spend a month on personal expenses. Then divide that by two or four, and that's how much you can take out of each check for these expenses.

Now if we were in a room together right now, you might look at me and ask, "Why don't you just take the total for one week and use that as your weekly total?" That would be a very good question. Here's a very good answer: your personal expenses are going to vary week to week. You may buy groceries one week that will last you for two, so you won't need to buy any the following week. One week you might buy cleaning supplies that will last you a month or so. You have to consider clothes in your budget as well. A shirt, a pair of pants, or a dress is not going to be a weekly expense, but that needs to be figured into the monthly total. The week you don't have to buy groceries is the week you buy that shirt or dress. Having that set amount every week helps you to stay on budget, which brings me to the next very important piece of advice: stay on your budget!

Make sure you set enough money aside from each check for your mortgage or rent. Make sure there's enough for the bills. Then stick with the amount you allotted yourself each week. If you don't have enough money to buy that over-exemplified pair of pants that week, don't use the credit card, and don't use money from the electric bill and promise to pay yourself back, because you won't! What you should also not do is *buy the pants*! I've said it before, and I'll say it again—the best way to save money is not to spend it in the first place. Wait until the following week and see if you have the money then. If you absolutely *have* to have the pants, then find a way to pay for it. Don't go out to dinner that week, or skip a few movies. Even take the money out of savings if you have any. It's better to do that than mess up your budget. Your budget is what's going to keep you from overspending, which, again, is the main problem with people who feel they don't have enough money. I've had times where I had to decide between going to a movie that weekend and buying a gallon of ice cream. I know it seems tedious, and I don't want you to have to nickel and dime your whole life, but you need to do that at least in the beginning to get yourself back on track and develop good fiscal habits.

I mentioned a savings account in that last paragraph. If you can start and maintain a savings account, then do so. You don't have to save a lot each week for it to add up quickly. Also consider putting part of your tax return, if you get one, into savings and any extra money you may earn. The temptation can be to splurge and spend it on a luxury item. That's fine to do, and you should—just don't spend all of it! The other temptation is to pay off some debt with the extra money. That does sound like the responsible thing to do. As much as you want to whittle down your debt, however, you have to remember that it's important to have some liquid assets available at all times. Many experts say you should have at least three months salary in your savings account at all times. I know for a lot of us that can be extremely difficult, but it's very important to have that backup in case of any financial emergencies.

If you're still not sure you shouldn't use the money to pay off debt, then let me explain it this way. You have already budgeted for your bills and debt payments, so those are being taken care of. If you stick with that plan and you're consistent, then you will eventually pay off your debt. It may not be as fast as you want, but even if you put any extra income toward the debt, you're not going to pay it off significantly sooner. It would take a lot of extra money to have a noticeable impact on your pay-off date. It will make an impact on your liquidity, though, and throwing all your extra income toward your debt leaves you without any emergency funds for things like car repairs, medical expenses, or losing your job. I have, in the past, been unemployed for several months at a time. However, during those times I didn't lose my apartment or car, go delinquent on any bills, or become late on any of my payments, because I had the savings account to back me up. So include in your budget a little extra money for savings.

Don't forget that with debt, like credit cards, your payments get smaller as you pay down the debt, so if you keep the same payment amounts, you'll pay off your debt progressively faster as time goes on. Even when there are months when it seems you're not making any headway because your payments just cover expenses that came up that month, don't worry. You may not have pared down that debt that month, but you didn't increase it either. When you start going in the other direction and increase your debt, then you need to start to worry. Remember that having some debt is not a bad thing. It can help you establish credit and raise your credit scores, as long as you keep it in control!

SUMMARY

- Keep track of not only your monthly expenses, but your weekly ones too in order to keep better track of your spending.

- Make a budget according to how much you take home per month.

- Stick to the budget!

- If you have to spend beyond your budget, find a way to pay for it (i.e. don't go out that weekend if you had to get a new tire for the car that week).

- If you possibly can, start a savings account and have at least three month's bills saved.

- Pay down the debt as soon as you can, but not at the expense of the budget or a savings account.

- Call the credit card companies and ask them to lower your rates if they are high.

- Consolidate your credit card debt to the lowest rate card and get rid of some others.

- If you can't pay for it with cash and you don't need it, don't buy it!

OTHER WAYS TO SAVE MONEY

Now we're winding down to the nitty gritty of saving money. If you've stuck with me through this book so far, you know we've talked about all the big stuff like food, clothing, credit cards, etc., and now we're going to talk about the many little ways you can save even more money—ways you may not have thought about or didn't think mattered a whole lot. A lot of these tips are things people usually don't want to try, don't have time to bother with, or don't think will do any good. But again, these are those little things that can add up to a lot! Even following one of these tips could probably save you the cost of this book!

GARAGE SALES AND ESTATE SALES

I absolutely love garage sales! You can find anything at a garage sale. And there is always a garage sale somewhere near you on any given weekend. The exception is in the Midwest and most of the northern United States, where we have to wait for more seasonal weather to go to garage sales. Garage sales are perfect for odds and ends and nick knacks, but they are also great to find tools, books, and even furniture. When I got my first apartment, half of my living room was furnished with things from garage sales and yard sales. If you're picturing that living room full of chairs with rips in them and stuffing hanging out or tables with dents and bad varnish, you're wrong. The key at a garage sale is not to buy just anything that's cheap, but look for really good stuff for next to nothing. I have two wing-back chairs in great shape that I got for ten dollars apiece and an octagonal end table cabinet for about five dollars. You have to take the time to hunt around for what you want and find it in good shape, but it's worth it for the amount of money you can save.

Other great things to find at garage sales are tools. A used hammer or screwdriver works just as well as a brand new one. If you want a brand new hammer, that's great, but if you don't really care if its new or not, then look for the tools you need at garage sales. You have to be more careful with power tools, because you don't know how much they've been used or if they're just about ready to break down. Sometimes, however, people just need to get rid of things for whatever reason, and they're practically brand new—like power tools! That can be the case for a lot of things at garage sales, not just tools. If you can find items that are still in the package unopened, then you've really found a deal.

Books are a great item to buy at garage sales. A lot of people read a book once and then they're done with it, so they throw them in a garage sale. If you don't mind a book that's been broken in a little, then consider buying books at garage sales. If you're like me, sometimes you want brand new versions of certain books that you like or want to collect, but if you're just looking for interesting reads, see what you can find at a sale. Sometimes at garage sales, I find paperback versions of books I own in hardcover. That way I can read the paperback and keep the hardcover book in good condition.

One thing you probably don't want to buy at a garage sale is clothing. You really don't know who has worn it or what it's been through. For me, it's just a little unnerving to buy used clothes. The other problem is that usually when people are selling clothes, it's because they're worn out or out of style. If you're looking for a cheap Halloween costume, then you can find great stuff at a garage sale. You can find vintage clothes for a retro costume or clothing, like old jackets, that you can alter into another type of costume. Earlier in this book, I gave you great ways to save on clothing, so I personally recommend sticking with finding good bargains if you want to add to your wardrobe. Remember, this book is about saving and stretching your money without sacrificing your quality of living.

Besides garage sales, there are also estate sales. At these sales, you find a higher quality of merchandise, probably at a slightly higher price. Even at that price level, however, it can still be a bargain. Estate sales are sales that are set up after someone has passed away or are moving and need to get rid of things. Estate sales are usually set up by professional services that specialize in these types of sales. Many have websites where they list sales for that week or month. If you search "estate sales" on the computer, you won't have any problem finding these sites or the sales directly. Newspapers are also still a reliable way to find estate sales. Because professional services handle these sales, you'll find that they categorize the items at the sale by the type of item or it's value, so you have a better idea of what you're buying. I'm sure you've heard those stories where someone bought a ten-dollar painting and found out later it was a Picasso—or how all those people on those antique shows end up with something worth twenty times what they paid for it. That really doesn't happen as often as it seems, but it can. At the very least you can find some very fine things for a very good price at these sales.

WORKPLACE BENEFITS

I talked earlier about taking advantage of retirement plans at your workplace, but you should also look into any other benefits, free services, or discounts that you're employer offers. The first obvious one is health benefits. Some places cover the cost of employees' health insurance, but if your job offers you health benefits where a small amount is deducted from your paycheck, take it! If you've ever tried to get medical insurance on your own, you know how expensive it can be for an individual, let alone a family. Not only are most policies cheaper through your company, but the policies themselves are usually better than you can get on your own. That can save a lot of money for you each month on premiums, not to mention saving medical costs, because you now have insurance. If you do have to contribute to your health plan, just be aware of how much is being taken out of your paycheck. Sometimes, but not often, you might be paying more through your work than on your own. All you have to do is check with a couple of insurance companies on how much a personal policy would cost you and compare it to what your work is taking out of your pay. Then you can know for sure if your work benefit is worth it or not.

Depending on the type of place you work at, like in retail, you usually get an employee discount of some sort. The discounts can range from ten to fifty percent or more if you work at any kind of retail store—like a clothing or grocery store. If you work for the airlines, you can usually fly free just about anywhere. If you can, make it a habit to shop where you work—not only for the discount you get, but you also help keep the patronage up where you work. Sometimes working at certain places gets you discounts at other places. For several years I taught at a community college, and because I was a teacher, I got discounts or free admissions to museums, theatres, and bookstores. A lot of businesses have agreements with other businesses to offer discounts to each other's employees. Take advantage of all these discounts, because they can definitely add up.

Find out about any services that your workplace provides. At both a college and a park district I taught at, they provided free use of their workout facilities. Think of how much it costs to go to a commercial gym, and that's how much I saved each month to workout. The school also offered use of computer facilities and use of the programs that they had. I know a lot of people have their own computers, but sometimes you don't have the programs you need. Some of those programs can be hundreds of dollars. Your other choice is to go to a copy place and rent time on the computers to use the software. Some of you may work at a service-oriented business. If you work for a tax preparer, you probably can get your taxes done for free or at least get some free advice that will in turn save you money on your taxes. If you work for a law firm, you may get free legal advice from one of the lawyers. They can charge hundreds of dollars just to talk to clients. Whatever the service your place of work provides, just be sure that your access and use of those services, especially if they're free, are allowed by your employer. If it's not allowed, then don't do it. There's no point in saving money if you lose your job.

Check out if your work offers help with tuition for college. Sometimes you can get full tuition paid if your education is work related. When I was a teacher, several of my students had agreements with their employers that the amount they were reimbursed depended on their grade for that class. An "A" was full reimbursement, and then it was less for each letter grade down. (That didn't put too much pressure on me!) If your work doesn't offer a program that covers tuition, they may help you with books, supplies, or transportation. It never hurts to ask.

Now let's look at retirement. I know a lot of you may not be thinking about retirement because it seems such a long way off, but you have to think about it! Now is the time to start putting some money away and investing it for the long haul. You need time for your money to grow. The first thing you need to do is find out if you have any kind of a retirement plan at work and if you're eligible to enroll. One of the things I've noticed over the years at the jobs I've had is that a lot of people are not even aware that there is a retirement plan at their jobs, or they don't care enough to find out about it. Even when they do find out about it, they don't enroll. It's usually the younger people that do this. They figure they won't be at the job long enough for it to be worth it. But a lot of retirement plans have stages of vestment where after each year of working you get a higher percentage of your retirement when you leave.

The other thing to consider is that you may be at that job longer than you planned. Many people think they're only going to be at a job for a year or so until something better comes along, and they don't invest in their retirement plan. Several years later they're still there for whatever reason, but they still never invested and lost all that time. So if your work has a plan and you choose to invest, try to invest as much as you can from each paycheck. At the initial enrollment you agree that a certain amount will be deducted from your check by your employer and are committed to that amount for the following year. At the next open enrollment at the end of that fiscal year, you can change the amount of money to invest and usually how you want your money invested. So watch for that paperwork every year and make sure you can commit to that amount for that year when you make the arrangements. You will find that once you budget for that deduction out of your pay, you won't miss it.

If your work does not provide a retirement plan, then you can always start your own retirement fund. One way that I chose was to start a mutual fund. A mutual fund is a collection of stocks from different sources, such as preferred and common stock, commodities, bonds, and other investments that are put into one huge fund. Then you buy shares into that fund. There are a plethora of different types of funds with different companies—I've been wanting to use the word *plethora* somewhere in this book. Success!—so I'll just give you a small sampling of some of those types of funds.

There are many companies offering mutual funds, so you'll have to do a little homework and some research on these companies to see how they've performed over the last few years. You'll want to look at the last ten years at least. After you find a company you like, you will then have to choose the type of fund you need. For right now I'm going to assume you're a young person who has maybe forty years until retirement. If that's the case, then usually an income fund is recommended.

Income funds are made up mostly of preferred stock, which is stock that is in strong, established companies that for the most part continually grow. This includes what they call "blue chip" stocks. Of course, at the time I'm writing this part of the book, companies are failing left and right, but there are still huge companies that aren't really going anywhere anytime soon, and these are the companies the funds invest in. These funds have higher capital gains and dividends that they pay out. If the companies are doing well, then they pay out more in capital gains and dividends, and if not, then you don't get anything.

Dividends usually get paid out quarterly and capital gains at the end of the year. Let me insert another handy tip here: arrange to have all your dividends and capital gains reinvested into the fund. You still have to pay taxes on both the dividends and the capital gains, even if you reinvest, but it is good to gain those extra shares every year by reinvesting. The most important thing to remember is not to worry about the fund once you start investing. Plan on being in this for the long haul. There will be a lot of ups and downs, but over a long period of time, these investments usually go up in value. At the time of writing this book, the market was hanging around the nine thousand mark. That's about six thousand less than it was a couple of years ago because of the economic crunch, but that's still over four times more than it was twenty-five years ago. If you had invested twenty-five years ago, you'd still be ahead.

Try not to think of your investments, whether its mutual funds or stocks, as a quick way to make money. You have to leave your money in there a while to see good results. It's never guaranteed that you will make money, especially in the stock market. There are companies that fail after decades of doing well, and people can lose everything. Fortunately, that doesn't happen as often as companies that continue to do well up to the time you're ready to sell. The longer you can stay in and ride the waves, the better chance you have of making money.

For those of you who are a little older, as my broker likes to remind me, you may need a more aggressive mutual fund, like a growth fund. These funds invest in companies that are relatively new and have potential for large growth in a short amount of time, as opposed to income funds that have more established companies where growth happens slower and in smaller increments. A growth fund is considered more risky than an income fund, because smaller and newer companies have a greater risk of failure, and you could lose money. They can, however, make large profits if the companies do well and expand. You need to have that potential for larger growth when you have a shorter period of time until your retirement. Hopefully the fund has a good fund manager. It's his or her job to buy, keep, or get rid of stock to maintain the profitability of the fund. These funds usually don't pay any dividends or capital gains, so the upside is you won't have to pay taxes on them.

Even though mutual funds are diversified, you should try to diversify the mutual funds you invest in. I have growth funds, income funds, and combination funds of income and growth right now. An income and growth fund has stock in both established companies and new companies. This way, you have the stability and security of the established companies and the potential for higher profits with the growing companies. These are considered mid-risk funds. There are also regular stocks to consider for your retirement, but since I know little about stocks and playing the market, I'll refrain from giving you any advice on that subject. You really should talk with a broker to find out what the best investments are for your particular situation. And when you do talk to your broker, ask about making at least one of the funds an IRA account. When you buy shares in an IRA mutual fund, it's the same as if you were contributing to a regular IRA account. Since IRA contributions are tax deductible, so are buying shares in an IRA mutual fund. If you make it a Roth IRA you can't take the deduction, but you won't be taxed on it later when you pull it out for retirement. Remember you have to be fifty-nine and a half before you can withdraw funds without penalties.

YOUR CAR

Your car can be a huge expense when repairs come up, especially as it gets older and, as we all know, even more so after you finish paying for it! The first thing you can do to keep your repair cost down is keep up the car. Get those regular oil changes and tune-ups to keep your car running smoothly and slow the wear and tear on the car. Tune-ups are relatively inexpensive, depending on what you need done, but oil changes are the most inexpensive service you can do for your car. Small expenses over a period of time are much better than big expenses all at once. If your car is under factory warranty, don't worry about having to take it back to the dealer for your routine maintenances, like oil changes. Factory warrantees recognize most corporate oil change places and brake shops, and they can be much cheaper than car dealerships. And if you don't have a warranty or it runs out, these places can also handle many types of repairs you may need on your car. They don't just do oil changes and brakes at these places. You can get a lot of different engine and mechanical repairs done that I can't even name because I don't know that much about cars. The reason I like to take most of my repairs to these corporate shops is not only are they a lot cheaper than an independent mechanic, but the company also has a reputation that you can count on. If anything isn't done right, they usually can take care of it right then and there for free and even throw in that oil change. Even if you can't get compensated with the person at the shop you went to, you always have the recourse to go to corporate and complain. With an independent mechanic if he doesn't want to rectify the problem, that's it. There is no one above them. I've always had good experiences with the chain shops, and they take good care of my little baby!

The time you do want to take your car to the dealership is when your car is under warranty. If anything goes wrong with your car, take it immediately to your dealership and have them fix it for free. Be sure to read the warranty and make sure what it covers, but it should cover just about everything, especially in the first year. Six months after I bought my last car, which was used, I realized the air conditioning didn't work. The car still had its factory warranty, so I took it in, and they fixed it for nothing. It would have been about six to seven hundred dollars to repair. That's six or seven hundred dollars that stayed in my bank account!

PUT IT BACK!

Now I know I've said this throughout the book, but it always bears repeating. The best way to save money is not to spend it in the first place. Before you buy anything, just stop and take a few seconds to think about whether or not you really need it. And if you do, do you need it right then, or can it wait so you don't have to use that credit card that you're about to pull out and use? How many times have you bought something and realized you didn't need it, want it, or use it. That's buyer's remorse. All you have to do is give yourself a little time before you decide to buy something or not. Walk away from it and ask yourself some questions. The most important one is, "Can I afford it?" That's really the crux of the whole problem, isn't it? It's what this book is really about. If you can't afford it, then you can't buy it. It's as simple as that. This is when patience is your friend.

Another good question to ask yourself is, "Do I already have something similar at home?" That usually comes up when I'm buying clothes. Many times I'll see something, such as a shirt, that I like, but then I stop and remember that I have something very similar at home. I put the shirt back and save that money. You can even stop and think about food and whether or not you really want it or are going to eat it. Think of your past habits. I know I'll see something that looks good and I'll buy it only to see it sit in the cupboard or the refrigerator and go bad before I even try it. I have to remember to ask myself if I'm really going to eat it or not. More times than not, the answer is no, and

I put the item back. With any of this, if you can afford it and you know you're going to use, wear, or eat it, then by all means, buy it. All I'm suggesting is that you give yourself a moment to step back and be sure that you really want it or need it.

Now if there is something you really want or need and it's just out of your budget, there is still a way to have it. No, I'm not talking about stealing. It's called Christmas! I don't mean to commercialize the holiday or cheapen it's meaning, but let's be honest here. You know your friends and family are going to get you something for Christmas, so you might as well give them a list of the things you actually need or want. If they're big, expensive items, you can suggest that several people go in on it. That saves them shopping and trying to decide what to get you for Christmas, and you get what you really want. This is how I got my TV, DVD player, VCR, and CD burner. Everybody is happy!

CONCLUSION

So you've stayed with me the whole way. I thank you for that. I hope what you've read can be really helpful to you. Even if you only use one thing from this book, it will probably be enough to cover the cost of this book, so at least you're even! There is nothing in this book that is either new or revolutionary. It's all about common sense. You have to live within your means. You may not like the means you have to live with right now, but you still have to be aware of what you can afford. That's how so many people have gotten themselves into trouble financially. People buy houses they can't afford or cars that have high monthly payments, and they're suddenly in over their heads. It's not, however, just the big things that get people in trouble. Like I've said before, it's the little things that will do you in just as quickly, and you won't know how it happened. People don't pay attention to the little things until they sneak up on them and put them into a massive financial hole. That's why the budget is so important. A budget keeps track of all your spending, especially all those small amounts that you forget about. It's the budget that steps in and says, "Hey, you can't afford that right now. Put it back!" Or it tells you, "Okay, if you buy that, you need to cut something else out to pay for it!" And sometimes it will say, "Go ahead and buy it! Since you stuck with me, you can afford it!" Listen to your budget!

Again, I know I'm about to repeat myself on these next points, but I don't think I can say it enough times. You have to be very honest with yourself when you're spending your money. When you have something in your hand at the store, you have to honestly answer the question, "Do I really need this, and will I use it?" The bigger question that you always have to be honest about is whether or not you can afford it in the first place! That's the tough one. People often think that they'll buy it now and figure out how to pay for it later. I speak to you from the future—don't do it! It's at these moments where you can save yourself a lot of money. Be honest with yourself, and you'll realize more often than not that you can't afford it or you won't be able find it in the budget to pay for it.

The last thing you need to ask yourself is whether or not you really want it. Here is where that blinding honesty comes into play again. Do you really want to buy that sweater or electronic device or that whozit, or are you buying it just for the sake of buying something? We all do it.

I'll be the first to admit that it makes me feel good to buy myself something. But if I feel guilty or have regrets later because I realized I really didn't want it or couldn't use it, then I've cancelled out that feel-good moment. I don't want to get into the psychological side of why we buy things, because I really don't know anything about that, but you should take a good look at why you buy the things you do. Maybe you're making up for a lack of something in your life or going through a bad period and you're using shopping as therapy. Like I said, I'm not an expert on that whole thing, but you might want to look at those things if your spending is getting out of control.

Take a time out. Even if you know you want something and can afford it, it's always good to stop and think for a second before you buy it. Of course, the best indicator of whether or not you should buy anything is how much you have to think about it. The longer you hesitate or think about it, the more likely it is that you shouldn't buy it. (By the way, this method can apply to any life decision you ever have to make.) Sometimes when I find something, even if it's something I know I want, I'll step back and continue shopping for a while and then come back to it when I'm about ready to check out or leave. If I still want it, then I buy it. Sometimes I find something else that I want more, or it may be better than the first thing I saw. Sometimes I go home and come back a few days later, and it will have gone on sale or have been reduced even further. Sometimes you have that feeling that if you don't buy it now it will be gone later. That's when people use their credit card when they shouldn't. I often put off buying things until I can pay for it in cash. Sometimes the item is gone by the time I get back to that store. Well, if you want to get cosmic about this, it's a sign that it wasn't meant to be! If that item is still there when I come back, then the fates are smiling on me!

Like I've said before, I don't want to be a killjoy about spending your money. If you know you want something or need it and you know you can afford it, then by all means, buy it! We need to help keep the economy going whenever feasible. I'm just asking everyone who reads this book to think a little more about how and why and on what they're spending their money. And this doesn't just apply to people like me with modest incomes who have to watch their budgets closely. I think people like Bill Gates or Donald Trump could benefit from this book. When you have a lot of money, you don't need to worry about how you spend your money, but if you ever have a reversal of fortune, you're going to need these skills to keep you from landing on your financial butt! And that's what this book is about. These are lifelong skills and practices that will help you when you're struggling economically and when you're doing well and living comfortably.

As I said in the introduction, this book will not make you rich. However, I think it can help you get out of a financial hole or prevent you from digging one in the first place.

It can also help you have more cash on hand when you need it. It's all simple advice that many of you probably already do or have thought of yourselves. I just put it all together in a book based on my own experiences to help you remember them. I'm sure there are things in this book that you may not have thought of at all. I hope you can use them as well. At least the ideas in my book don't have you selling off your home and moving to a cheaper state or switching jobs or liquidating assets to invest in some long-term something or other. Everyone can use these ideas, whether they're rich or not so rich, and different things will work for different people. Some of the things I talked about in the book may not work for you. That's where you apply your own experiences and modify what I've talked about in the book to fit your life.

That's why living within your means is so important. What you can afford is unique to your needs and your income. I know people who make two and three times as much money as I do, and they're struggling to make ends meet. I am completely baffled by this. If I were making their salaries, I'd be swimming in the dough! That's because they are either living beyond their means or right up to their means. That's a key point to remember. Even if you can afford everything you spend money on, if you are right at the precipice of your means, you have no wiggle room for unexpected things. You should always give yourself that wiggle room, because you just don't know what will happen in the future.

How many celebrities have you seen over the years who, when they were successful, bought huge mansions and expensive cars that they could afford at the time, but then when the career and money went south, they went right into bankruptcy? They didn't plan ahead, and they pushed the envelope with what they could afford. Now if any of those famous people had bought a more modest but nice home and a nice but less expensive car and invested a lot of their fortune at the time they had it, they could still be sitting pretty. The same rule applies to us, my friends. Think ahead to the future when you're making your budget. Assume that things could get financially worse, and plan for that possible scenario. If we all became more responsible with our finances, this country would be in a lot better shape economically. We can do it!

Thank you again for buying this book and taking the time to read it. Emerson once wrote, and I paraphrase, that if you help someone else breathe easier because you were there, then you have been a success. I hope this book does help you breathe a little easier, at least financially, and I truly hope that it will help you. And if you do find that you suddenly have extra money on a regular basis, think of it as giving yourself a big raise! You deserve it!